SAVE ROOM FOR REAL ESTATE

A GUIDE TO MAKING MILLIONS IN THE REAL ESTATE INDUSTRY

NESAHN ROBINSON

REACH REALTY GROUP PUBLISHING

SOUTHFIELD, MI

Nesahn Robinson/Reach Realty Group Publishing
17200 W. 10 Mile Rd Ste 201
Southfield, Michigan 48075
www.reachrealtygroup.com

Save Room For Real Estate/ Nesahn Robinson -- 1st ed.
ISBN 978-0-692-85321-4

Cover Art By: Brad Foltz
Book Edited By: Mike Valentino

To my mother. Thank you for unconditional love along with your full support in all my endeavors. I am forever grateful.

IF YOU WANT TO BE A MILLIONAIRE , FIRST ASK YOURSELF IF YOU ARE WILLING TO MAKE SACRIFIECES IN ORDER TO ACHIEVE YOUR GOAL.

—SAVE ROOM FOR REAL ESATE

CONTENTS

CHAPTER ONE

WHY REAL ESTATE

So, let me guess, you picked up this book in hopes of making millions of dollars in the real estate industry. You want to be a millionaire I take it. If you read this book from cover to cover, then exercise what you learn, there's a good chance that you may accomplish your goal of becoming a millionaire. The first rule of thumb, and this is by far the most important rule to know, is: Wealth starts in the mind. Before you can ever be wealthy in the physical state, you have to be rich in the mental state. This will attract people, places and things to all accrue when needed. You will think it's perfect timing every time things go your way. Truly, it's just you manifesting your reality.

Try to remove all negative people out of your life. They
will only drain you of much needed energy. Now I'm not saying to go and quit your job tomorrow because you hate your
boss. What I am saying is to look at your circle of influence.
The people who you willfully allow to be in your life. Remove
all the naysayers, the people who always look at the bad
things in life instead of the good. These will be the people
who like to spread bad news. When they talk, it's usually
about someone's downfall. These are the cup half-empty
people. Surround yourself with the cup is halfway full people!
These are positive thinking individuals who rarely speak
on the negatives of the world.

Surround yourself with people who believe in you. The
ones that will say, "I know you can do it!" This might mean
you losing contact with close friends and family members.
There is nothing ever gained without sacrifice. The more you
want to gain in life, the more you have to sacrifice. Look at
the majority of millionaires and billionaires. For the ones who
are self-made, most will tell you about the long hours they
worked every day to get to where they are now. They will tell
you about marriages that broke up because of their work,

and unbalanced households because they were never at home, barely knowing their kids and what they were up to. Friendships lost because they fell well below the limited free time one had to spare. Missed opportunities to spend with loved ones that passed away due to being overworked and driven for success. These are all sacrifices people have made to get to where they are in life. Most will see these people and think they're lucky. They want to be rich like these successful individuals, but most are not willing to make the necessary sacrifices.

So, if you really want to be a millionaire, first ask yourself if you are willing to make sacrifices in order to achieve your goal. If you are, then trust me, you must start by removing negative people out of your life. After you have removed all negative people out of your life as much as possible, now you have to know what you want out of life. It's time for you to set some goals. Set small goals and set extremely large goals. If you shoot for the moon and come up short, you still land on the stars.

After you have finished this book, decide which route you want to take to get to your financial goal. Then set your overall large goal you want to accomplish. Be realistic in the time frame you give yourself. For example, you can say, "I want to be a millionaire in the next seven to ten years. I want a net worth of over ten million dollars over the next twenty years." Then set some very small goals to get there. It can be as simple as calling a real estate school, finding out their pricing for class and when the next class begins. It can be calling a property management company and asking if they're hiring. See if you can intern for free there. Make a small goal to attend an open house that has been remodeled. Look at all the detail work that goes into a rehab house flip. Call a real estate company and ask if you can shadow a Realtor for a week so you can see the daily tasks of a real estate agent. Once you have achieved one small goal, set more small goals. For example, set a goal to become a real estate agent. Then set a goal to have more sales in your first year than any other agent have had in their first year with the company. You keep setting more and more small goals until you realized you have achieved your large goal.

One key component that will help you achieve these goals is to visualize yourself achieving each goal you've set for yourself. Take time out each day to visualize your goals. Visualize the small goals as well as the large goal. See your self in that state of being a mutli-millionaire. Visualize the house you will live in. The cars you will drive. Visualize your bank statement. Visualize everything you want to happen for you. It's best to do this in the morning or at night before you go to bed. This will keep you focused on your goals, as well as let the universe know what you want in your life. The real estate industry is like the dessert in life. Many people will find out about all its opportunities late in life. The great part about the industry is that it's never too late to start a professional real estate career on all levels.

Real Estate is property consisting of land, houses and build-ings, as well as all the natural resource under it and above it. This includes crops, minerals, diamonds, gold, water and air rights. Real Estate is also the business of buying, selling, or renting land, buildings or housing.

Now let's answer an equally important question: why should I be participating in real estate? The answer is be-cause most of the rich people in this world are involved in real estate in some manner. If you wanted to be a pilot and you found out that most pilots around the world know how to speak Portuguese, only a fool wouldn't start learning how to speak Portuguese. That is a fool and someone who was not serious about being a pilot. The problem is the majority of people want to be rich but only a few will actually put in the time and effort that it takes to become rich. You will read several different stats about this. For the most part they all have in common that up to 80% of the world's millionaires made their fortune in real estate in some manner. That's right, up to 80% of the world's millionaires acquired their wealth in the real estate market. Now surely only a fool wouldn't start learning the real estate business! That is if he or she wanted to be a millionaire. Same rules and principles apply as the pilot and the Portuguese language referenced earlier.

To know something, however, is one thing but to master it is another. By no stretch of the imagination should you believe that by studying real estate you're going to automatically become a millionaire. That would be insane to think so. As with most things, it's what you do with the knowledge you learn that will dictate if you become a millionaire or not. To be honest, some people lack self-discipline to become successful in any career. Let alone to become a millionaire at doing something where the odds are highly stacked up against you. Some people want to be able to just get by with a couple of creature comforts.

Many people would be happy with just a roof over their head, three daily meals to eat and one vice of their choice. So, although many want to be rich only a few have the mental toughness to do so.

There are thousands of ways to become financially well off. By no means am I saying that this is the only way to become a millionaire. I'm not here to tell a stock broker his clients will never become rich using his services. Nor would I ever tell a twenty-five-year-old man or woman with hopes of still making it to the pros that he or she would never play the sport professionally. I'm not here to discourage anyone from their dreams of choice. Although I am here to show the odds of becoming successful at your choice. If your focus is on becoming rich, then you need to start learning the real estate business and fast. By all means, go after your dreams of becoming a professional athlete. Go after your dreams on becoming a rich and famous actor, singer or dancer. Or whatever it is that you want to be in life. But understand that many people in this world are not going to achieve the goals that they set as a child. It may take one to be in their late twenties to early thirties before one will realize that they need to make another plan of action in their life. Most will

keep the dream of becoming rich near to heart and that's
when I hope they find this book. What you will learn is that
no matter what you tried to do before to become a millionaire, if it was not in real estate, the odds were enormously
stacked against you to succeed at your goal.

Just think about it. Let's say you went to a professional basketball game, and at halftime, you were selected to
come down and shoot a half-court shot for a million dollars.
You were given two options to select. You could choose line
one where you get two shots to make it in for a million dollars. Or you could choose line two where you get eight shots
to make the basket and win a million dollars. I think you
would choose line two where you get eight chances to try
and make it in the basket. It's the same situation where picking anything but real estate to become a millionaire. It's as
though you are picking line one to take only two tries at making a basket to win a million dollars. I bet you almost
everybody would choose line two in this situation. If that's
the case, why do so many choose line one in life? Line one
represents any other measure to becoming rich outside of
real estate. Next time a friend or family member tells you
about their newest get rich quick idea, you probably will be

looking at them and their idea a little differently now. That is if it's not real estate related.

Each and every day more people are becoming aware of the fruits that real estate bears. You have television shows that keep popping up that are real estate related, one after another that keep coming. From people flipping houses to Realtors selling houses and everything in between. This has been great in a lot of ways and bad in others. Great because it allows more people to understand and recognize that there is another way to become a millionaire other than just the childhood dreams of becoming a rock star or becoming the next Michael Jordan so to speak. Bad because they have also misled the majority to believe it is a get rich quick and over-night industry. Let me tell you right now: it's not. What it allows for is with appropriate use an opportunity to become financially well off. Yes rich, the term most people love to hear. First understand, however, that for just about all of you, it will not happen overnight. It will not be an easy task. There will be hard times and setbacks. If you stay strong and focus through the years, I am sure you will reach whatever goal you have in mind for yourself. So, if someone asks you while you are reading this book,

"Are you thinking about getting into real estate?" you can confidently say, "Why, yes I am."

Many of times you will come across the seasoned investor who will tell you his or her story. Good or bad they will quickly share if they were fortunate in making millions or not. Gain more energy with all the success stories you hear. Try to quickly block out all the horror stories that are told to you. Fear has a way of stopping people dead in their tracks. I'll help take away some of the fear by telling you this. You will take losses in your real estate endeavors. Some ways that you will take losses are, you may have your property broken into and stripped of the furnace, hot water tank, plumbing pipes and electrical wiring. If it's a house they may also steal appliances, windows, bathroom vanities, even toilets. I have seen all these items stolen out of property before. You can have an eviction that takes four months to complete. You can have a house that you plan on flipping catch on fire with no insurance on it. This personally happened to my friend. I've watched and personally helped people make millions of dollars over the years in real estate. Sadly enough, I've also watched them all take losses as well. Everybody's built differently, and timing a lot of times is the deal maker or breaker.

If you take a twenty-thousand-dollar loss in real estate, after years of making hundreds of thousands of dollars in real estate, then the lost can be considered as just the cost of doing business. If you take a twenty-thousand-dollar loss in your first year of doing real estate, you might leave the industry alone altogether and tell your horror story to anyone who will listen. No matter what you do in life the common denominator to your success will always be consistent. So, regardless the area of real estate you decide to go into, prepare yourself to give one hundred percent effort in your work. Be the first to arrive to work. Be the last to leave. Just wanting something is not enough. You must give your all at accomplishing your goal.

Don't be afraid to fail, doubt kills more dreams than failure. Understand that no matter how much you know or think you know, there is always something new to learn. In fact, everyday comes with new lessons to learn. Even with over eleven years of real estate experience, I myself am certainly open to learning.

I have spent more than four years as a property manager, and more than six years as a real estate agent. I have also spent more than three years as a real estate broker and owner, and more than eight years as a landlord. I have helped clients flip houses for over four years. I have dealt with title companies for over seven years. That is a pretty good resume of real estate experience. From all those years of work I will give you the tools to be successful in real estate. I will tell you the good, the bad and the ugly side of the real estate business. Try to always view the positive side of each aspect of the real estate business. If someone becomes rich as a property manager, so can you should be your approach.

I only mention the negatives to be realistic and not sell anyone a dream of peaches and cream of the industry. Alot of people think they know all about the real estate industry, but if you ask them a simple question like "who is the largest real estate holder in the world?" they will not know the answer. Try it on the next person who says they are real estate savvy. The answer is McDonalds!

Now, there are hundreds of ways to use the real estate industry to secure your financial freedom. You have professional builders who build commercial and residential properties and make millions in the process. This is true, but it takes a very large sum of money to get into the driver's seat of this profession, and I will not steer you into becoming one. Most construction company owners were multi-millionaires before opening or taking over the family

business. Nonetheless, I do not want to discourage a newly licensed contractor who has dreams of building new hotels and other buildings in your downtown. I would say, however, to take it slow. Start your company and build up your name by offering home improvement and home remodeling. You can also specialize in a certain area of home improvements like flooring. There are companies out there that make millions of dollars selling and installing hardwood floors.

I can name hundreds of ways to make money from the real estate industry. Alot of people would not connect the dots to a successful plumbing company, electrical company, roofing company, or heating and cooling company that makes millions of dollars yearly as real estate related. The fact of the matter is, all these businesses must credit their success and millions of dollars to the real estate industry. That is why the percentage of millionaires who have earned their millions from real estate is so high. These sectors of the real estate business are very self-explanatory so I will not get in-depth in each of the areas. Just remember that with any sector of real estate that you go into, hard work and sacrifices will be a toll that you will need to pay to achieve financial freedom.

CHAPTER TWO

If It Makes Dollars, It Makes Sense

There is a quote many people use in determining if they should seek out a new financial venture. The quote is, "If it makes dollars, then it makes sense". That is the reason why a lot of people choose their dream job. Ask someone if they would still want to be an actor for a living if they were only to make a fast food worker's pay. Many would say no I would not. So, it's not being an actor that you really want to be in life. It is to be rich while doing something you love. The ancient Chinese sage Confucius writes, "Choose a job you love and you'll never work a day in your life." This is what we all start out in life dreaming of doing. For most people the harsh reality is that they will not end up doing something they love for a living. The unpleasant truth is they will be chiseled down to looking for a job to make funds. Once hired, time has a way of moving very fast. Then they start letting go of their dreams very slowly, to the point where there is no more hope. That' s when you hear people start to talk about being realistic. Some keep a small piece of hope tucked in the back of their brain. You see them in the casino and the lottery lines to name a few places they go. They play the lottery in hopes of winning the huge Powerball prize. They utter their hopes and dreams with quotes like, "You have to play to win".

The lottery was designed for the poor. The casinos were designed for the middle class. Both are in the dream selling business. With long lines of participants waiting their chance to instantly become a millionaire. Then they can buy their happiness back they assume. For all the gamblers out there, skip to the next chapter if you don't want to hear this. Don't worry, I give you time. The truth of the matter is gambling is by far the worst way to try and get rich. Most lottery winners suffer an ill fate of some kind. You see, the way the universe is set up you have to become the person before the physical will appear. You want to be a millionaire then act like a millionaire. Talk like a millionaire, walk like a millionaire. Eat like a millionaire, master a craft like a millionaire. Invest like a millionaire and I promise you, you will be a millionaire someday. If you're blessed to have a millionaire family member, friend or associate, don't ask but beg for them to be your mentor. If you're worried about pride just remember pride usually comes before the fall.

So many people think they need to reinvent the wheel in order to be successful, but it's not true. Success is like a roadmap. If I ask you to drive five states away from where you are now, without a map, would you know how? Yeah, there's a small chance you can get there without one. That portion of people are all in that twenty percent category. Now if someone gave you a roadmap to get to your destination, your odds of reaching that destination would increase dramatically.

When you find a mentor who will teach you what they did to be successful, that is your map to becoming successful or shall I say rich. Do as they do, follow directions to the smallest detail, and humble yourself to understand how and why they are where you want to be in life. This did not happen by accident. They had to learn a lot of life lessons that they could teach you if given a chance. If they agree to make you their apprentice, understand they are now your roadmap to success. I'm pretty sure somewhere down the line they will explain to you how they are involved in real estate to generate some income.

For the rest of you readers who do not have the luxury of knowing a millionaire who will mentor you into wealth, let this book be your guide to wealth. Let this book be your mentor and roadmap to success and financial freedom. A rule that I want you to follow from this day forward is to never take advice from anyone that you wouldn't trade bank accounts with if you had the option. I was blessed and fortunate enough to have my immediate family all invest in real estate. Me being the youngest sibling of four, I learned a great deal from my mom, two sisters and brother. I learned that the sooner you invest in real estate the better from my mother and sisters. I learned if you don't invest in real estate you will grow to hate the mailbox from my brother, who was the last of my immediate family members to invest in real estate. I was blessed to have been given several pieces of real estate. I was young at the time and did not understand the power that I had received. I lost one parcel to the county for unpaid property taxes. I came a hair shy of losing the other as well to the county.

This was around the time I became a real estate agent. Yes, a Realtor. I never in my life thought I would be a Realtor for a living. I had hopes and dreams of playing professional sports not selling houses. So, why did I decide to become a real estate agent? I decided to become a Realtor when I found out eighty percent of the world's millionaires made their fortune in real estate. So, I figured hey if it makes dollars then it makes sense to me. I wanted to submerge myself in everything that was real estate. I wanted to sell real estate. I wanted to buy real estate. I wanted to flip real estate. I wanted to be a part of the eighty percent of millionaires who derived their wealth from real estate. I wanted to be a millionaire. Yes, I wanted to be rich. I gave myself a realistic goal of becoming a millionaire within ten years of my real estate start date. I have been truly blessed, and by the end of my sixth year in real estate, I have a net worth of over one million dollars. Yes, I've done it. I've become a millionaire!

One of the reasons for my success was my savings method. You must start an aggressive savings method. If you already have the funds to get started you're in luck. If not, you must start saving your money. The old saying "it takes money, to make money" is correct a majority of the time. Start saving at least twenty percent of all earned income that you make. If you feel you can't afford to do so, look at your monthly bills and start cutting back. Turn off that cable television and save the cable bill money. Besides, do you want to watch millionaires on television or be a millionaire? Stop going to the hair salon or barber shop. Do your own hair. Pack a lunch to work every day. Clip coupons when you go grocery shopping. Buy your clothes from the sale rack. My point is you can find a way to save twenty percent of your income. Now here is the key on what to do with your savings. Do not touch the savings account funds unless it's for an investment that has a high probability of making you more money in real estate. In order to have success in real estate, you have to prepare for the opportunities that will present themselves.

Success is just opportunity meeting preparation. Growing up, me and my oldest sister and brother were very careless with our money. We spent our money on instant gratification items. Ice cream truck comes down the street, if we had money we bought ice cream. New fashion line item comes out, if we had the money we bought it. One of our favorite musical artists comes out with a new CD, we bought it. I mean the last thing that was on our minds was saving money. If you would've asked us what saving was, we would have told you, "When someone saves your life or saves someone else's life." This is funny but very true.

However, this was very untrue with my second oldest sister. In fact, it was the exact opposite of her behavior. For get talking about valuing a dollar -- she valued a penny. I mean literally a penny. She would say" pennies add up to dollars." She valued money at a very early age. She would not buy ice cream off the ice cream truck very often. Instead, she waited for our mother to go grocery shopping and bring back ice cream. She did not go out and buy the latest fashion trends. Nor did she go out and buy the latest new CD or cassette out. Instead, she would wear our oldest sister's designer clothes when needing to impress. She would watch the music video channel instead of buying the actual CD or cassette.

What did she do with her money you ask? She saved it. I mean, boy, did she save her money! I can recount at a very young age her loaning people money. I mean she was in the sixth or seventh grade giving out loans. I'm not talking about five or ten dollars here. I'm talking about a couple hundred dollar loans. It's been said that the hardest thing to do is save money. Its also been said that the easiest thing to do is spend money. I believe both of these statements to be true. However you must master the art of saving if you do not have the capitol to start investing in real estate.

I can not stress enough the importance of saving your money. Now the secrete rule! Once a savings account is established.Never spend any of your money saved unless your buying assets that will make you more money. My sister mastered the art of saving at a very young age.

This skill of saving that my sister had, allowed her to always take advantage of really great deals that come forth. She kept this saving skill into her adulthood. When she became an adult she found real estate fast. I mean fast. She bought her first house at the age of nineteen. She went on to buy other houses for investment purposes and became a landlord. My mom bought the house we all grew up in and taught me and my sisters and brother the value of homeownership. However, it was my sister who introduced the family to the real estate industry. She has also introduced many family and friends to the real estate business as well. Now my sisters and brother, mother and myself all own multiple real estate properties apiece. We own over twenty-five collectively. I started out my property managing career working for my sister. When she reached the tenth house owned, she hired me as her property manager. This was my first introduction to real estate. I learned how she would buy houses and how cash was king. I learned how there are always good deals out there, you just have to be prepared for when they come. If someone came to you this very day and said they had a family emergency back home located in another state or out of the country, and they asked you to buy their house that was paid off for forty thousand dollars and you knew it was worth eighty thousand, would you have a payday on your hands or would you be the one to say, "Wow, that's a really great deal" and then try to sell the property to someone else who might throw you a couple dollars for the referral. This will be the difference between you making tens of thousands of dollars or possibly hundreds of dollars.

You have to save twenty percent of your income to be prepared for great deals like this one. This is actually a true story by the way. Early in my real estate career I was in a situation where someone offered me the opportunity to buy their house for half the value. They were originally from out of town and had a family emergency and needed to move back ASAP. I did not have the funds at that moment and someone else bought the house. I was unprepared for the opportunity at that point in time. A similar situation happened again years later. That time, I was prepared, and I bought the house. I went on to sell the house for double what I paid. That was years after I started to save twenty percent of my income. That allowed for me to have the money on hand to buy that property.

CHAPTER THREE

The Starting Point

So, now you're ready to embark on a new adventure in life. You have decided that you want more out of life than sub-standard conditions. You want to be in the upper class and you've convinced yourself real estate will take you there. This can be very true for you but first you need to decide what category of real estate you're going work in. There are several divisions of real estate that you can go into to make millions of dollars. The first way that I will talk about is becoming a Real Estate Agent. When you decide to become a real estate agent, you are unplugging yourself from the matrix. Reason being is that you are now in control of your income bracket. You will get paid on your worth to the world. Unlike W-2 workers who can tell you with a drop of a dime how much money they make a year. Just ask a W-2 worker and they all know the answer. They will tell you, "I make fifty thousand and year." "I make thirty-five thousand a year." "I make a hundred and eighteen thousand a year." Yes, they are all plugged in very securely to the matrix. On January 1 of each year they know how much money they will have made come December 31. The great position you're in when you become a real estate agent, preferably a Realtor to be exact, you hold your financial freedom in your own hands. If you tell family and friends on New Year's Day that you will make a million dollars for that year, no one can call you a liar. Just think about that. You can say, "I will make a million dollars this year" and everyone has to look at you and know that it is possible for you to do just that.

I personally think the hardest part of being a real estate agent is not knowing when you will be getting paid. There is an old saying us agents share. We say, "Do not count your money, until you can count your money." What we mean by the phrase is, you never know when you're going to get paid. You can have a house under contract, have a closing date all set, and then the closing doesn't happen. Unlike other jobs where people know they're getting paid on a specific day, real estate agents only hope things go as planned. Most of the times things do go as planned and you get your check. However, there are other times where you get blindsided by events out of your control. I once had a closing, and the day of the closing most agents perform what you call a final walk thru of the property. This was a house set to close. We went by and discovered that someone had moved into the vacant house. They stated that someone had leased the house out to them. Needless to say, the closing did not take place that day. Luckily, I was able to get the family to move to another house and the closing took place at a later date.

This has happened to me personally about three times in my career. There are a group of scammers out there that will find vacant real estate properties for sale. They break in, change the locks, and post ads on advertising sites like Craigslist claiming that the house is for rent, at a usually under market value. They do this to rent the house out very fast. People come by the property to view it. Then they pay the crook thinking he/she is the landlord, to only find out days later that they were scammed. You can also have your closing delayed and canceled altogether because of vandalism. You get under contract for a house or commercial property and while under contract, crooks steal everything possible from the property. I have seen properties get burglarized for furnaces, hot water tanks, central air system, kitchen cabinets, refrigerators, stoves, dishwashers, microwaves, copper pipes, electrical wiring, windows, tubs, sinks, toilets, bathtubs, doors, and yes even bricks. Bricks, who steals bricks from a house? It's a shame, these kinds of terrible incidents all delay and even cancel out deals. You feel bad as an agent that you will not be receiving a check. But you always feel even worse for the owner of the property that was vandalize and robbed, especially when they do not have insurance on the property. You can hear it in an agent's voice when they have a scheduled closing and the file doesn't close on the day it's set for. You know that agent probably told someone I'll pay you on Friday, anticipating a closing and a check that does not turn out. It can be stressful for a lot of agents who fall in this category.

Now, to become a real estate agent you must first go to real estate school. Depending on what state you live in the hours that need to be completed vary. Check with your state to find out the exact number. Once enrolled in real estate school you will learn all the laws that govern real estate agents for your state. You will learn about your fiduciary duties to your clients. You will learn that you have to work for a brokerage. You will learn all your responsibilities and obligations to the brokerage that you join. You will be taught everything about real estate from vacant land sales to commercial sales as well as residential sales. You will need to complete your state mandated hours of school and pass all your courses. Then you will schedule to take the state mandated test, and once you pass, you will be a licensed real estate agent.

If you haven't decided what brokerage you're going to go work for this is the time to do so. Real estate school prices vary from state to state, though most range of $250-$750 for the tuition fee. The state exam cost varies as well but most fall in the category of $70-$150. When deciding what brokerage to join I recommend interviewing with at least three different brokerages. The more the merrier if you ask me. Most real estate agents do not realize at first how big of an impact this decision will have on their career. In many cases, it's the difference between success and failure. So many newly licensed agents go join a popular, name brand brokerage, believing that name and fame is going to help them out tremendously. In most cases, it doesn't. When buyers and sellers decide to buy or sell they invariably pick an agent with whom they feel comfortable. Most couldn't care less what brokerage you work for. They are choosing you as the person to represent them in their real estate transaction.

Also, please note that you need to decide what type of real estate you are going to specialize in. Are you going to be a commercial sales agent? These are the agents who sell commercial buildings, like the buildings you will see in your downtown or your local hardware store, restaurants, supermarkets, apartment buildings, etc. Commercial real estate agents sell these properties when a company or owner wants to sell. Most commercial real estate agents do not sell a lot of property each year. Mostly one to three a year. They can still make good money, however, because the selling prices are usually much higher. If you only sold one parcel in a year, that might sound bad, right? But what if I told you the building sold for twelve million dollars? The commission paid to your brokerage was three percent of the selling price. That's three hundred and sixty thousand dollars!

When you work for a brokerage you will have to split some of the commission with them. The commission split is negotiated when you join. Let's say you're on a 70/30 split your way. That means for that one deal you would have received a two hundred and fifty-two-thousand-dollar check. That one deal doesn't seem so bad now does it?

What makes the world of real estate so beautiful is you're supposed to close four deals like that one in a year. That would earn you over One Million Dollars for the year. Believe it or not, there are indeed agents out there who make this type of money a year. Then you have residential sales agents who sell the houses and condos you see in your neighborhood. Same rules as commercial agents apply for what the earning potential could be. They have television shows about real estate agents who sells high end homes. Thus, they make millions of dollars of yearly income. Most agents, however, will not sell high end homes. If you fall in this category, you must work your way up to multi-million-dollar sales agent status. Let's just stop for a moment and think. How many careers can you pay less than a thousand dollars to join, and then gives you the option of making millions yearly? Not many that's for sure!

There are other real estate agents who make millions yearly by selling a large volume of houses. They sell in bulk to investors and make large commissions. Then you have the agents who sell lower end houses. They make their millions by selling a lot of houses yearly. It's the quantity vs. quality method. You can become very rich by perfecting either craft. Remember, of course, that it will cost you more and more money to make more and more money as an agent. It's no secret that the real estate agents who make the most money, also spend the most money in advertising. Start to pay attention to all the real estate advertisements you see and hear. This will give you a good idea on all the ways real estate agent market themselves. What you will notice is a lot of agents advertise in multiple ways. In fact, the top agents advertise in just about all the various ways. You will see their television commercials. You will hear their radio ads. You will see their billboards around town. When you google home buying or selling they will pop up on your screen. You will start thinking wow, this person's everywhere. Think about this question. Why do you think McDonalds spends billions of dollars each year in advertising? The company is one of the top five recognizable brands in the world. Why are they still spending so much money on advertising? The answer is: "So they can remain a top five recognizable world brand".

So, don't think you can spend a ton of money in one or two months and then just stop your marketing. The marketing you did to make the money, will be the same marketing you should do to keep making that amount of money and even increase it. When you want to make more money, spend more money on advertising. They have a direct effect on one another. You just have to choose what type of agent you're going to be and master it. This is one avenue in real estate that can turn you into a millionaire. Just become a real estate agent to get started with the process.

Now, I'm not going to say it's a piece of cake to attain millionaire status from being a real estate agent. However,It is very possible. Someone who works as a supermarket cashier can never say they will become a millionaire from bagging groceries. No offense to the cashiers of the world, I'm just using them as an example. A majority of all the professions you can pick for a career offer little to no chance of you making a million dollars in one year. They don't even put you in position to build wealth so that someday you can be worth a million dollars or more. Being a real estate agent does give you the opportunity to one day make a million dollars or more in one year. It also allows you to build your wealth so one day you will become a millionaire.

When you become a real estate agent and you have closings, that's when you get paid. The great part about being a 1099 worker is you get all your money with no taxes taken out. This allows you to deal with a higher amount of capital than most W2 workers. So, let's say you build your brand up to the point where you're having six closings a month. The average sales price of the property you're selling is three hundred thousand dollars. You receive three percent commission off each property; that's nine thousand dollars for each closing. No taxes taken out, just your split with your brokerage. Let's say you're still on a seventy/thirty split your way. That's sixty-three hundred dollars you will receive for each closing. You're doing six closings a month, so that's thirty-seven thousand and eight hundred dollars a month. If you worked as a W2 worker and taxes were taken out immediately at a thirty percent rate, that would be eleven thousand, three hundred and forty dollars you don't have for investing each month. That's one hundred thirty-six thousand dollars yearly that is not in your control. With this extra capital you could make wise investments such as flipping a house that would bring you in a forty percent profit. This would decrease the amount you had to pay to the IRS by forty percent.

On top of that, the money you make off flips is taxed at a capital gains tax rate of fifteen to twenty percent. That will be less than your earned income taxed amount. Also, remember, you're only paying taxes on the forty percent profit you made. You will be able to deduct all expenses incurred. If you decided to buy a rental property with the extra money, you could get on a payment plan with the IRS and have a portion of the rent money allocated to pay your monthly installment payments with them and you still will be making extra money. If property values rise in the area where you bought your rental property, you will be winning on both ends.

The key to becoming a millionaire as a real estate agent is not to work yourself up to the point where you're making a million dollars or more a year as an agent. It is for you to build yourself up to where you are making six figures as an agent, then you save twenty percent of your income and after a couple of years you use your real estate knowledge to become an investor yourself. Now, it's great if you can work yourself up to making millions a year as a real estate agent without any investments along the way. You can do it, it's definitely possible, but the majority of millionaire and multi-millionaire agents I know all became millionaires before they stated making millions a year, and they all became so with smart investments. So, if you want to become a millionaire in the fastest amount of time as a real estate agent, be ready to invest in real estate as well.

CHAPTER FOUR

Get Paid to Do the Easy Work

There's actually a way to make millions of dollars in the real estate industry without selling any real estate at all. All you have to do is start up a title company. Title companies are the companies that real estate agents/brokerages hire to close transactions between buyers and sellers when a real estate agent finds a buyer and seller who agree to a set of terms to sell a property. No matter if the property is a vacant land, commercial property or a residential house, the title company handles the transferring of ownership from one person or company to another. They ensure that the person selling the property is in fact the owner. They also make sure that all the liens on the property are paid at closing. Liens are unpaid bills that get attached to the property, such as a mortgage loan, unpaid water bills, unpaid property taxes, home financed repair work done on the property, etc. If you get sued and there's a judgment against you, the courts can place a lien on your house as well. This is the reason many investors put their real estate assets in a limited liability company name, also known as a LLC. Some investors will go so far as to put every property they own in a different LLC name. This separates each home from one blanket lawsuit over all their property. It also will keep any lawsuits coming in from a property to be directed toward the LLC and not you as an individual.

The title company makes sure none of these liens are on the property. If there are liens on the property at closing, the title company makes sure the seller pays them off. They issue the buyer what is called a warranty deed at closing. A warranty deed is insurance on the deed. They issue a warranty that there are no liens on the property unless stated and understood beforehand. If you have a warranty deed and a lien shows up on your deed that was not stated, the title company has to pay that lien off. This is the most sought after deed which I recommend you receive when doing any real estate buying or selling.

There is another deed that the title company will issue if someone does not want to pay for the warranty deed, or in some cases where someone is willing to inherit all the liens on the property. They can issue the buyer a quit claim deed. This is by far the worst deed to receive when doing a business transaction. The title company only transfers ownership of the property to a new person or company. They do not guarantee anything about the deed. Not even that the person selling the house is the owner. This deed is so bad, a lot of individuals create quit claim deeds themselves to sell property, since the title companies are not going to give any insurance on a quit claim deed. They figure why pay the extra money when they can do it themselves. Quit claim deeds were never created for business transactions. They were created to pass ownership of a property from one loved one to another, like a mother or father giving one of their children a piece of property. It has become more and more common, however, that people handle business deals with quit claim deeds. There's a joke out there that one guy quit claim deeded another guy the White House. It's a funny joke but that's just to say how unreliable a quit claim deed can be.

When a title company first starts off they need to get a processor and an underwriter. The processor is someone with years of experience doing research on deeds. They know how to follow the chain of ownership of a property. They can read when liens were added on to a property and taken off. Finding a good processor is key to starting up a title company. They are the essential key to running the business. Finding a good processer will not be easy. Most of the time, new title companies offer a higher salary to current processors at other companies to get them to switch companies. You may have to do this when starting your title company. Also, remember this when you do have a processor and your company is growing. You need to be increasing your processor's salary as well. If not, you could fall victim to your processor leaving your company for a higher salary at another title company.

You will also need an underwriter to back your warranty deeds. The underwriter is a larger title company that gives the smaller title companies insurance policies on the warranty deeds they issue. For example, if you own a title company, when you close a file, you may charge a thousand dollars for title insurance on a property. Out of that thousand dollars you will have to pay your underwriter three hundred dollars to insure the file. If there is an error that comes up at a later date for that file, the buyer will call you to correct the problem. You would then turn around and call your underwriter to correct the problem, and the underwriter would be liable to pay for the errors.

The commission splits between the smaller title company and the larger underwriting title company are all negotiable. The more errors you have the lower the commission splits the underwriter will be willing to give to you. If you have way too many errors occurring the underwriter can stop underwriting your title company altogether. This would be really bad for you because there are not many underwriters in each state. Most states will have between two to four of them. If one cancels your policy with them, you will almost certainly get blackballed from the title world. They all will ask you on your application has another underwriter canceled your policy with them. If yes, please explain.

No business wants to take high risks of losing money. So, the other companies most of the time will deny you. It's very important, therefore, to not make too many mistakes as a title company. A lot of title companies in their early years will not close any file without the underwriter first reviewing the file. This is a way to double check to make sure a file has

no errors before closing it out. For the seasoned title companies, they will only submit files to underwriting that they feel
are questionable. When problems arise (because in business
there are always problems) most title companies will pay the
small errors off themselves. This will reduce the amount of
reported errors to your underwriter.

Title companies have rules and regulations that they
all must abide by. Each state's rules and regulations can be a
little different from one another. One rule that is enforceable
in just about all the states, however, is that a title company
cannot pay a real estate brokerage or agent any money for
business. This restricts title company owners and employees
from telling real estate brokers and agents that they will pay
for business. In most cases, the real estate broker or agent
picks the title company with which they want to close their
files. So, title companies have to win more business by out-
performing other companies. They will explain how they can
close deals faster than the next company, and how their fees
are lower than other title companies. They will make their
office as nice as possible for the agents and their clients. They
will offer refreshments when you enter such as water, soda,

chips or candy. They will give away pens, mugs, calendars, key chains, etc., lot of the little stuff that makes the client and agent feel welcomed while at their office.

The hardest part by far about owning a title company is trying to convince brokers and their agents to use your services. In most real estate offices you will find representatives stop by from different title companies all thru the year. Depending on how big the real estate brokerage is the more the title reps will stop by. Most agents find a title company early in their career and stay loyal to that company. A lot of real estate brokers only allow their agents to use the title company of his or her choosing. It is not against the law for a real estate broker or agent to actually own a title company themselves. When doing so, the agent or broker must have the company address separate from their real estate office address. The title company has to close other agents' files from other brokerages. The title company cannot be limited to the files the real estate agent or broker owner provides.

Another problem that title companies face are the scammers. Years back, all the title companies would allow a buyer to bring in a certified check to closing. They changed their rules after banks started allowing picture depositing.

What the scammers would do is go to the bank, get a certified check, and then go to the closing and right before they enter the title company, they would take a picture of the check and with their cell phone re-deposit the check into their account. The title company would then close the file with the check. They'd deposit the check, and days later the check would bounce -- after they had recorded the property in the scammer's name. People were actually scamming title companies out of house and home literally!

In every industry, there are crooks and thieves. This is a problem title companies have faced in the past. As technology gets more and more advanced, scammers will come up with more and more ways to scam people. Just like real estate companies, there are a lot of title companies in each and every state. So, it will take time and patience when growing your company. The good news is as you grow it will be a steady growth. There are many small title companies with five to seven staff members out there making millions of dollars yearly. I personally know a few owners myself. Once again this is not some get rich quick overnight thing. The owners of these title companies have worked very hard for several years and even decades to be in the current circumstances they're in. If you are willing to dedicate your-self and make the needed sacrifices, you can be one of them too. Have you ever seen an infomercial, where there is some guy telling you how you can get rich with his real estate sys-tem? He goes on to say how with his real estate system can make you millions of dollars with no money down. All you have to do is buy his DVD or audio system for five hundred bucks to learn how. He then goes on to show people who have used his system to make very large sums of money. Well, if you have seen these infomercials, the system that all these guys are talking about is wholesaling property.

The majority of wholesalers stick to residential prop-erty sales. A wholesaler is an unlicensed real estate individual who sells real estate for a living. In most states, it is legal to sale real estate properties, up to five to seven properties a year. After a person sells more than five or seven properties, depending on what state you're in, they must have a real es-tate license to sell any more. Most wholesalers disregard this law because it is very hard to prove. Title companies will process a deal for a wholesaler in the same manner as they would for a licensed agent. Wholesalers act in a lot of ways like a real estate agent. The major difference between the real estate agent and wholesaler is the real estate agent has a state license. They are also bound by state laws, rules and regulations. Wholesalers are not.

There are many wholesalers out there who do not want to get a license. They feel that the state has too many rules and regulations by which to abide. So, they go off the grid and sell property. This is the reason most real estate agents will not do any business with a wholesaler. New to the business real estate agents, however, oftentimes will do a deal with a wholesaler. That's if their brokerage allows them to do so. For those agents who do business with wholesalers, they find out very quickly not to do a deal with a person who has nothing to lose. I have seen agents do deals with whole-salers and the deal fall apart. The wholesaler states that the title company is holding an earnest money deposit. The title company confirms to the agent that they are. When the deal falls apart, though, the wholesaler sends the title company a mutual release that has been forged with buyer and seller names on it. The title company hands the wholesaler the earnest money deposit back. The agent tells his client they will be awarded the earnest money funds for the buyer's breach of the contract. Then the agent calls the wholesaler because he has stopped replying to his/her emails. The wholesaler ignores the calls. Finally, the poor agent calls the title company to verify that they still are holding the earnest money deposit. Only to find out that they are not, and they have docs signed by all parties to the deal. Now the agent is left wondering what to do. Their seller thinks they are entitled to funds that no longer exist. Keep in mind that your typical earnest money deposit is between one thousand and ten thousand dollars. Now the agent calls their client to let them know what happened, and at that point most clients take it out on the poor agent. Some will go as far as suing their brokerage for the funds. All of this is why licensed agents only work with other licensed agents. Let a licensed agent try these same actions. They will have the state all over the case. Licenses will be lost and the agent can face fines and even jail time.

There are some wholesalers who will protect their name and never do such a thing. What the successful wholesaler does is take advantage of the laws. If they are allowed to sell up to five or seven houses a year without a sales license, they make the most out of it. They make sure they clear a ten to twenty-thousand-dollar profit off every house they sell. If they sell five at a twenty thousand dollar profit, that's a one hundred thousand dollar a year job.

This is what they do to make ten to twenty thousand dollars off sales. They put up signs all over town that read "I Pay Cash for Houses". They advertise in the city paper, as well as on the Internet on sites like Craigslist. They put flyers all around town. Then people call you wanting to sell their houses. They go view the property. They check the comparable sales of properties, not just the one in question. Then they will offer the seller about half of what the house is worth. Their main objective is to find disputes where people are looking for fast cash. There are a lot of good people who end up in bad situations and need cash fast. It might, for example, be a young man who just inherited a house from his dying mother or father, who would rather have twenty thousand dollars today instead of forty thousand dollars in three months. There's a long list of people who decide they want to sell a property and fast. Those who are drug users and people with gambling problems, just to name a few more.

After a wholesaler finds someone who is willing to sell their house for an agreed upon amount, the wholesaler does one of two things. They purchase the property at a very fast rate. Typically, within seventy-two hours of acceptance.

This method is used when they are buying a property at an unbelievable price. They want to close fast so the seller doesn't change their mind. They know if they take too long the seller can come into money another way and decide not to sell. The seller could find someone else who will buy the property and sell it to them. Most wholesalers are not going to sue a seller if the seller decides to not sell them the property, even if the seller signed documentation to sell to them.

This is the opposite of real estate agents. So, in situations where they find a really great deal they close fast on the transaction. After they have purchased the property they market the house for sale on sites like forsalebyhomeowner.com and Craigslist. Some will even list the property with a real estate agent. However, this is rare. When they do list with a real estate agent they ask for an exclusive agency listing. This allows an agent to market the house for sale and earn a commission if they find a buyer. It also reserves the right for the seller to find the buyer themselves and pay no commission.

After the buyer is found the wholesaler can make very large profits off the sale. The selling price does not have to be large for the wholesaler to make good money. They can purchase a house for twenty thousand dollars, then sell that property in a couple of weeks for forty thousand dollars. It may seem very simple but it's not. Wholesalers work hard to find the steals and deals out there. But the old saying is true: hard work does pay off.

Another method wholesalers use is the no money down purchases and sales. This is the method you mostly hear on the infomercials, where they will teach you to buy and sell houses with no money down. This is the process where the wholesaler follows the same steps to acquire a seller. This time the seller is not a person looking for fast cash, but rather a person looking to sell their property. The seller has yet to call or list their house with a real estate agent as well. The wholesaler sends the seller an offer to purchase the property, and the seller accepts the offer. The wholesaler will put in the purchase agreement that they have sixty to one hundred days to close. They will make the closing date even farther out if the seller allows them to. In the purchase agreement that they have the seller sign, they will include verbiage that this contract is assignable. This means they can sell their rights to buy the property to someone else.

After they get under contract with a seller to purchase the house, they go about finding a buyer to assign the contract to. They then market the property for a higher sales price. This will be their profit made from the sale. When they find a buyer, they send the file to a title company and set up a closing date. They will inform the seller the day of the closing. When the title company draws up the closing docs, the seller will notice that there is a new buyer name on the docs. They will see the original buyer name on the docs being paid an assign fee. This fee will be the amount the wholesaler marks the sale price up for. The file closes and the wholesaler walks away with potentially thousands of dollars without ever putting up one red cent.

There are wholesalers out there who make tons of money. The bad part about wholesaling is a lot of times the sellers feel used and taken advantage of in the end, when they sell their property to someone, to only watch that same person make no repairs to the property but then sell it for thousands of dollars more in a very short period of time. Some get mad enough to sue. Most of the times the seller never wins in court, but it might at least make the wholesaler want to split some of their profits with the seller, if the wholesaler has already been sued more than seven times in one year.

Not to bash wholesalers, because in all fairness there are very successful wholesalers out there with high morals and standards. It is rare but there are wholesalers who will tell the seller upfront that they will be assigning the contract to another buyer. Some will even ask the seller to list the property with their company. If a wholesaler markets his/her company right, most sellers will not ask if their company is a licensed brokerage. Nowadays, if you have a good-looking website people will believe you are a professional company. The highly successful wholesalers actually create a company. In fact, if you decide you want to be a wholesaler, I definitely recommend you have a company. Make sure your website is very professional looking. Dress the part, too; perception is reality. Study the real estate market so you're always in the loop of recent sales in the area you're working. Find a title company that you trust and build a long-lasting relationship with them. If you use the knowledge that you acquire and are willing to work very hard, you can indeed be quite successful as a wholesaler.

NESAHN ROBINSON

CHAPTER FIVE

Reserved For the Elite

Many people have the preconceived notion that real estate is only for the elite. They feel you need to be rich to have anything to do with real estate. This is so not true! When I first started in real estate I was far from rich. As a matter of fact, at the time I considered fifteen hundred dollars to be a very large amount of money. I did not have thousands of dollars to buy any real estate at all. I had bad credit to go along with that. Yet, everything starts with the mind. You must first believe in yourself. Close your eyes and visualize what you want and who you want to be. Then you can make it happen. It does not matter where you are in life. If you want to be successful in real estate you just need to want it, that's all.

For all of you who do not have large amounts of money to start flipping houses for profit, I recommend becoming a real estate agent. Your funds will come in large amounts, which makes it easier to save money for flipping houses or becoming a landlord. There are several ways to get rich in real estate and you can get rich by mastering any one of them. If you want to increase your odds and make the process faster, I recommend doing at least three of them. Become a real estate agent and sell property. Become a landlord and rent out property. Become a real estate investor and flip houses. Master one or all fields of real estate and write books, and hold seminars teaching others how to be successful at it, too.

I recommend picking three of the four options and you will be on the fast track to becoming a millionaire. For wealthier readers who are looking to get into real estate for the first time, you have a huge head start in the opportunities available for you. You can skip right into becoming a landlord or a house flipper. If you choose to become a landlord, the first thing you need to do is hire a really good Realtor. Secondly, you need to hire a property management company. There's not too many investments you can make that will yield as high a return on investment as real estate. When you begin your property buying process do not limit the search to just your local area. Do your homework to find the most valuable properties for rental income. When I say do your homework that goes for both nationally and internationally.

Your real estate agent will find you the properties that match your preference. Your property management company will find you your tenants. Most property management companies charge a fee of ten percent of the rental amount for a monthly fee. They will also charge you for tenant placement as well. This fee is usually around one month's rent. They will also charge you for repairs that are needed to the properties. I recommend stating to your property managers that you want before and after pictures sent to you for all repairs done on your properties, if they do not do so already. You will also want to ask how they perform their tenant screening process. You can add or take away any process you feel is needed to their pre-screening of tenants for your property. Remember they work for you and not the other way around.

If you decide to flip houses do your research on the market where you're looking to flip. Talk to your real estate agent. Ask for comparable sales of properties that you're thinking about buying. Your agent should be able to show you comparable properties that match the one you're about to buy. Do your math on the comparables to get the difference between buying and the possible resale amount. The resale amount to purchase price should be equal to or less than fifty percent of each other. Then you should hire a licensed contractor to give you a repair rehab quote. The repair quote must be equal to or less than twenty percent of the resale value. This will make your purchase and rehab budget equal to or less than seventy percent of your possible resale value. You will typically need to pay 6% on the sale price of the property in real estate commissions when the property sells. You will also have to pay a title company to handle the closing. These fees and prices are based on the sale price as well. The seller's fees are higher than buyer's because in most cases you will need to pay for a warranty deed to give to the buyer at closing. This is insurance on the deed that there are no liens on the property that are not stated at closing. The real estate agent's commission and title company fees should be equal to or less than ten percent of the purchase price. This will leave you a twenty percent profit on the flip.

However, you want to be sure your numbers are right. If not, your holding costs will slowly eat away at your profit margin. Holding costs are the expenditures necessary to maintain the property until it sells. These will include the electric bill, water bill, snow removal or grass cutting bill and a home insurance bill. You do not want the property to remain on the real estate market for a long period of time. These bills can add up over time.

One way to increase your sales time on your flips is to remember these three rules. Never short change the budget on the kitchen rehab. Never short change the budget on the bathrooms, and never short change the budget on curb appeal. These are the key items that sell a house. Everybody wants people to look up to them with admiration. What more admiration can you have for a person than when you pull up to their house. A house is typically a person's pride and joy when it comes to material items. When people see the outside of a person's house they come to a conclusion about the person. Whether they think the person is rich, upper middle class, middle class or poor. That is why you make the outside presentation its best. If the outside is decorated lavishly, it will make onlookers believe the owner is one level higher than they probably are. This is a high selling point.

The reason you never cut budget costs on the kitchen, is because kitchens are the number one selling point for women. Not to say that men aren't moved by a great looking kitchen, too, but statistics will show the number one selling tool for women is the kitchen. If a couple is married, nine times out of ten the wife will be the determining factor for the purchase. If she falls in love with the kitchen you just made your Realtor job alot easier. The goal is when the flip is finished to get it sold as fast as humanly possible. So never short change the kitchen budget whenever you're doing a flip.

For the bathrooms, the reason you never cut the budget or be cheap with the rehab cost, is because this is the one place everybody in your family will use as well as guests. I have heard some people say no one's allowed to cook in my kitchen but me. However, I've never heard anyone say that their guests cannot use their bathroom. The bathroom is very important because it allows a person to feel comfortable when handling their most sensitive hygiene needs. These three areas should take up at least fifty percent of your flipping budget.

Also, keep in mind that over pricing a property is a sure way to have it sit on the market for a long time. So, make sure your numbers are right. If you have a good real estate agent, they will get the numbers right for you. Don't make the costly mistake of biting off more than you can chew. A lot of times when a new investor is halfway done with a project or just finishing up, they start looking for their next flip. Some will even buy their next rehab flip before the first one is sold. This can turn into a costly mistake if you don't have the manpower. The old saying "good help is hard to find" is true. You might get very lucky and find a great set of contractors your first try. In all likelihood, you're probably not going to be so lucky. That means it will take longer than expected to finish up your flip. If you buy another house before the first one is sold, you increase your holding time expenses for two houses now instead of one, as well you're more inclined to have vandalism to the properties the longer they sit empty.

You may decide you don't want to use the same contractors for the second flip. If you already bought the second house, this will pressure you to hurry up and pick anther contractor for the job so you can decrease your holding cost. But this may put you back in the same position as the first flip. Take your time when deciding on what contractor you are going to select. Ask to see their before and after pictures for the projects they worked on in the past. Ask them how long it took to complete each of the projects. Ask if there were any changes in the original rehab quotes to previous clients. If yes, then ask the

SAVE ROOM FOR REAL ESTATE·69

reasons why. This is of paramount importance. Why? Because with a quality real estate agent and quality contractor by your side, you will be well on your way to flipping enough houses to become a millionaire.

CHAPTER SIX

Growing Pains of Being a Landlord

One area of real estate that is widely used is renting out property to tenants. I would say about eighty-five percent of millionaires have property they rent out to tenants. This makes them a landlord of that property. There are several ways you can become a landlord. You can rent out residential houses to tenants. You can rent out apartment units to tenants. You can rent out condos or co-ops to tenants. The main difference between a condo and a co-op is, in a condo you own the property and have a deed. In a co-op, you own an equity percentage in the building like a stock.

You can also rent out commercial properties that include retail stores, such as stores located in a mall. There are also standalone buildings such as your local drug store, hardware store, restaurants and convenience stores to name a few. You can even rent out vacant land. This would be a situation where the landlord could rent the vacant land to carnivals coming into town, business parking lots and farmers for farmland to name a few.

Many people do not realize that even hotel
or motel owners are landlords. They have rules and
regulations they must abide by as all landlords do.
The rules and regulations that landlords are required
to abide by are slightly different depending on what
state you live in. Most of the rules and regulations
are the same with structural properties. Here are the
most common rules and regulations:

You need to provide a safe and secure property. There can be no safety hazards present in the
dwelling. That goes for the electrical system; all wires
and outlet plugs must be up to city code. All the light-
ing fixtures have to be up to code. The furnace or
boiler heating system and hot water tank must be
properly installed and up to code. The plumbing system needs to be up to code. The property must have
at least two ways to enter and exit the structure. All
windows must be able to move up and down. While
up, the window must be able to stand up on its own
and not immediately fall right back down. There can

be no tripping hazards inside or outside the structure. The roofing structure must be up to code. All doors must be able to lock and unlock properly. There cannot be any double sided key locks on any residential doors of the property. If the property is a commercial property it must be handicapped accessible as well.

So, you're about to purchase your first piece of real estate to become a landlord. The very best advice I can start off giving you is to not financially need the rental income. One sure way to go into the real estate business and go right back out will be if you need the money for your daily living expenses. I see it happen all too many times where someone wants to replace their income from one source to real estate. I can promise you this, if you become a landlord for over five years you will encounter an eviction you must perform.

An eviction is where a tenant is behind on their rent or have breached their lease agreement with you and you want them out of your property. Examples of a breach would be a tenant moves in

more people than you allowed on the lease. They
may add an animal to the property without your con-
sent. The tenant can be physically damaging the
property more than normal wear and usage to name
a few. When you are faced with an eviction most of
the time it will affect your money being earned.
Moreover, it will cost you to perform the eviction.
Out of pocket cost could range from one hundred
and fifty dollars all the way up to three thousand dollars. Every state's procedure and fees are different
and prices will vary. If you're not performing the eviction yourself the cost of hiring an attorney or having
your property manager will vary as well.

So, imagine the new landlord who just purchased three new residential houses to rent out to
supplement his or her income for retiring. Then this
owner has to do two evictions on the three properties purchased in the first year of becoming a
landlord. Let's say both eviction procedures cost
three thousand dollars each of out of pocket cost,
and both took two months to complete. Let's also say
the evictions were for non-payment of rent. Both
properties rented for one thousand a month. This

new landlord is out six thousand dollars of out of pocket cost and four thousand dollars of projected rental income. Furthermore, there is still the cost of paying your property manager or real estate agent to find you new tenants for both properties. You see, if you really need the money and a situation like this occurs, most will sell off their properties and say real estate is not for me. They don't want the hassle of renting and being a landlord.

Now, on the other hand, if you do not need the money for immediate use and this same situation occurs, you will simply chalk it up to the cost of doing business. You will understand that being a landlord is a marathon not a sprint to becoming rich.

Some other hardships that you may face include vandalism to your property. This will increase your insurance cost of the property if you file a claim. It can also take a hit on the profits if you repair the damages out of your pocket. The great and wonderful thing about being a landlord, however, is that you get to make money in your sleep. Very few people become rich actually physically working for money. For most, you need to make money work for you. Becoming a landlord is one way you're making money work for you. For the most part if you are supplying adequate housing and you address any needed repairs that arise with the property, you will receive your rent money in the stated timely manner of your lease agreement. So, once you have just one rental property you have now started to make money in your sleep. The more rental properties you own the more money you're making in your sleep. It will feel good to retire for the night and wake up in the morning a richer man or woman than the previous day. Most millionaires' and billionaires' biggest assets are their real estate properties. Most millionaires will have small residential and commercial rentals in their portfolio. Examples include single family home rentals, small commercial buildings and vacant land to name a few. Most billionaires will have high end real estate. Examples include residential mansions, golf courses, luxury hotels and commercial buildings large in stature.

I definitely recommend that you become a landlord fast if you're not one already. Remember when you buy a property you own the mineral rights to that land. If there's natural gas, oil, diamonds or gold under your property, all of that belongs to you. You also own the air rights. All the air above your property belongs to you as well. Even if it's not touching your property, no one can build anything above your property without your permission. When you do become a real estate owner, never forget that you now own one of the best assets on earth. That is a piece of earth itself.

Now if you have little money for investing in real estate and you do not want to be a real estate agent, there are other ways to get into the real estate business. You can still become a landlord by doing what I call the two in one method. You can buy or get financed to buy a multi-unit house like a flat or duplex. You live in one unit and rent the other unit out. If you have a mortgage, you use the other unit's rent money to pay the mortgage and you save the money that you would have paid for the mortgage in a savings account. When you have saved enough, buy your second rental property. Now you will have another income streaming coming in without a mortgage. Save the monthly rent from that property and keep saving the money you would have been paying for your mortgage with those funds. You will save the amount to buy another house in half the time it took you to buy the second house for cash. Keep this process up and by the time you reach ten to fifteen rental properties in your portfolio you will be a self-made millionaire or close to it. Just continue the process until you are a millionaire and your goal will be achieved. You will now be considered by most as a rich man or woman.

Another way of achieving this goal is becoming a property manager. This process takes a little longer to achieve but you can achieve the goal nonetheless. To be a property manager you will need your real estate license. Unlike commercial or residential sales agents, a property manager does not sell real estate at all. Hiring a property manager takes away the headaches of managing rental properties. Yes, it can be a headache at times. The more properties a person owns as rental property the more likely they are to hire a property manager to manage the

property. They will not have time to go by one of
their properties to make repairs when needed. They
won't have the time for tenants to be calling them
while they are at work requesting repairs to be
made. So, they hire a property manager to take care
of any issues the tenant may need to be resolved.
Your duties as a property manager will include tenant
placement, collecting rental payments, evictions and
fixing all needed repairs to the property. In some
case with apartment buildings the property management company will be responsible for grass
cutting, snow removal and parking lot upkeep as
well. Property management companies usually
charge ten percent of the monthly rent of the property. They will also have a set fee amount for
properties as well. Sometimes the rental rate is too
low to only charge ten percent. They also typically
charge for each repair that is performed on your
property. They will take before and after videos or
pictures as proof of work performed. Some landlords
will have repairs be approved by them before done.

I once had a client who was the worst to
work for. He would call me whenever one of his

tenants didn't pay their monthly rent. We would have a polite phone conversation about it, then later that same day he would text my phone extremely long text messages about the tenant. He would use vulgar text language describing what he would do if the tenant continued to not pay. He would insult the tenants, calling them harsh words such as poor, trashy, uneducated, and dummies to name a few. The really harsh words I'd rather not say, but you can use your imagination to understand what I'm saying. The guy had split personalities. After receiving the text message, I would call him and he would be the same polite guy on the phone. Really creepy, needless to say. When that contract was over, I did not renew it. I stopped property managing for him the first chance I got. As a property manager, you just never know how some of your clients will turn out to be.

When you're a property manager you must have a team in place. You will need a minimum of two licensed repairmen with one always on the clock. You need an accountant, too, along with a lease representative and someone to handle evictions. Some

of the bad things that can happen to you as a property manager include tenants being unruly, giving you
and your staff a hard time. Tenants assaulting you or
staff. Owners talking to you with little or no respect.
Owners demanding to be let out of their contracts
early. The worst things that can happen to you are
situational events. For example, let's say it's 11
o'clock at night on a ten below zero night in January
and a tenant's furnace goes out. They call your twen-
ty-four-hour emergency hotline number and inform
you of the problem. They tell you to send someone
over right away because they have kids and a new-
born baby in the house. You call your contractor
who's supposed to be on call for the night but he
does not answer. The tenants call back and complain
it's taking too long, it's been over an hour and no one
has arrived and it's freezing cold inside the house.
You keep calling and calling your contractor but he
does not answer. You call your other contractor
who's off work and he says he can't go fix the furnace
tonight. He states that it's his wife's birthday and
they're spending necessary time together. He say's
sorry but he can't help right now. Your next move,

you try outsourcing the job find to anther contractor.
You get no luck. No one is willing to go out at one
o'clock in the morning in the blistering cold to repair
the furnace. The tenants decide to heat up the house
with candles and the stove. A candle falls and catches
the drapes on fire. The fire engulfs the house and
sadly someone dies in the fiery blaze.

If this event happened, you would be in a lot
of trouble. That's something to think about. This is an
example of a terrible situation that can possibly happen if you're a property manager. There's a lot of
liability in being a property manager. Nonetheless,
there is a great side to being a property manager,
too. When you become a successful property manager you get the perks of making more and more
money each year. As investors buy property and see
great returns on their investment, they will buy more
and more properties. This equates to you making
more and more money. The really successful property management companies have hundreds to
thousands of properties they manage. This equates
to hundreds of thousands of dollars to millions of
dollars being made monthly. Yes, that's right I said

monthly. You can build your team up to hundreds of members. This will lessen the chance of situational events happening to you. This is another way to become a millionaire in real estate. Like many who have done so already, become an elite property manager and you can become a millionaire in the process.

CHAPTER SEVEN

Being Responsible for Everyone

I'm sure you've heard of the big name real estate companies out there like Century 21, Keller Williams and Re/Max to name a few. Well, these companies are actually called brokerages. brokerages are state licensed real estate companies who operate in real estate transactions. They can handle all forms of real estate sales transactions. From land sales, commercial sales and residential sales. The state requires that every real estate brokerage have a licensed associate broker run the brokerage. In order to become a licensed real estate broker in most states, you must work as a full-time real estate agent for at least three years to five years. You must have a vast amount of experience as a selling agent and buyer's agent.

Every state is different with their mandates. Some states will allow you to have enough qualified real estate experience to become one. Once you have the qualified experience in real estate, you will need to go to real estate broker school. After you graduate from broker school you will need to take a state mandated broker test. Once you pass this test you will be officially a real estate broker. This gives you the power to run your own real estate company. You can start your own real estate company and run the business. For example, if your name is Bob you can start up Bob Realty. You just need to make sure the name is not licensed in your state already. You can buy a franchise like a Century 21, Keller Williams or Re/Max and operate it yourself.

When you decide to become a real estate broker and open a real estate office there are some things you need to know. You will hire real estate agents to work for your brokerage. They all are required to have a broker's license like yourself or a real estate sales person license to work for you as a real estate agent. Most real estate brokerages hire their agents as independent contractors. This avoids the company having to offer their agents healthcare, dental and vision insurance. It also allows for you to not offer a 401k plan as well. In most real estate offices, the real estate agents split a portion of the commission that is earned with the brokerage. The commission split is a negotiated split amount. Most splits will range from fifty/fifty all the way up to flat fee monthly pay and a hundred/zero percent split. It just depends on what package you're offering.

When you hire an agent you will have them sign an independent contractor's agreement contract. This contract will state a lot of variables. The variables could be the commission splits, employment time frame, company rules to follow, referral splits, office time of use and insurance you must keep to name a few. Most brokerages make their agents carry errors and omissions insurance. This protects them and the brokerage from lawsuits that could occur while doing business. Some examples of the not so pleasant requirements of being the broker of the company are: you are responsible and liable for everything that goes on in the brokerage. That means every sales transaction, no matter if you or your agent sold the property or land, you are liable for any and everything that goes wrong. As the broker, all your agents work on your behalf. So, if you have an agent doing something he or she should not be doing, you are responsible for it. If one of your agents gives bad advice you are responsible for it. If one of your agents steals from a client, you are responsible for it. If your agent drives a client to a showing and gets into an auto accident, you are responsible for it. I think you understand where I'm going with this. As the broker, you are responsible for the actions of everyone who work for you. The liability and fault is and will be always on your desk if a problem occurs. If an agent is at fault for anything that draws a lawsuit, best believe your brokerage will be sued. To be a broker and owner you need to be a very good problem solver. You will get daily problems dropped on your desk and it's your job to resolve each and every matter. If you're not a good problem solver and cannot resolve issues before they become legal lawsuit issues, you will more than likely be out of business very soon.

Another problem you will have as a broker is gaining real estate agents to work for your brokerage as well as keeping them there. It is a very competitive business with hiring agents. Brokerages are constantly marketing and recruiting agents to come work for their brokerage. If you have a good sales agent, they will go after them. They will offer them, for example, better commission splits and less office fees to get them to switch over to their brokerage. For the agents at your company that are not making good sales, they will go after them for recruiting as well, offering them better training and more buyer and seller leads to join their brokerage. This can cause a loss in agents as well. Where this really hurts is if you have a good agent at your office making good sales and they decide to leave. This will surely affect your income. If you lose too many agents too fast you can be out of business pretty soon if you have a high overhead cost. One way to prevent all of this is to have a great overall employment package to offer your agents. This will make it hard for your agents to leave your brokerage if they're going to get a below, same or a little better of a deal to switch companies.

The wonderful part about being a real estate broker and owner is that you duplicate yourself in your earnings. You will now be making money off every deal your agents close. You can have your agents pay you a monthly fee to work for your brokerage as well. You can do one or the other or both. You can grow your brokerage to be one of the biggest in your city, state and even the country. You can then franchise your company name, allowing other people to pay you to use your name for business. Once you have a successful real estate company you will be making six to seven figures of yearly income. That's hundreds of thousands of dollars up to millions a year.

Another great part about owning a brokerage is anyone can do it. You will just have to go out and hire a broker to run your company. This will affect your profit margin so I recommend becoming a broker yourself. Once you have your company running like a well-oiled machine you can go on vacation

and come back to checks on your desk. Many successful real estate brokers become millionaires
before they retire. So, if you like problem solving and
have great people skills, become a real estate broker
and owner and master the craft and you will soon
enough become a millionaire. Let me ask you a question. How do you eat an elephant? It seems like a
hard question, right? But it's actually an easy one.
The answer is "one bite at a time". The meaning behind the statement is that you have to start whatever
goal you're trying to achieve. No matter how big or
small the goal may be, you have to start. Procrastination is the killer of dreams. People come up with
multi-million dollar ideas that they let go to waste
due to procrastination. Have you ever had a great
idea that you knew would be a hit...to only procrasti-
nate long enough to forget about that idea? Then
months or years later you see your idea in a store or
on a television commercial. Odds are you probably
have had this happen. This book can tell you one way
to get rich or one thousand ways to get rich. The
truth of the matter is, it will not help you at all unless

you actually apply what you have learned from the book! Decide what you are going to put into action and then do it. The elite are and will always be the doers. You can't be afraid to fail. The most successful people are the ones with the most unsuccessful ventures. If your objective is to become a millionaire, real estate will dramatically increase your odds of becoming one. It did so for me, and it can do the same for you. The END!!!

Now this is the part where you're saying, "ah", wait a minute. You never told me how real estate turned you into a millionaire." How could I forget such a thing? Well, it all started when I learned and comprehended just how large of a percentage of the world's millionaires received their income from real estate. Once I learned this, I made a plan to learn all the ways to make money from real estate. After learning that there are hundreds of ways to make millions off real estate, I narrowed it down to three categories that presented the highest percentage rate of obtaining my goal. I decided that I would become a master at the three areas of real estate. One: To become a very successful real estate agent. Two:

To become a real estate broker and owner. Three: To become a landlord. So, I enrolled in real estate school and studied like my life depended on it. I wanted to acquire all the knowledge that real estate school provided. I studied every night. I talked to myself with motivational words. Like, "you're the best, you're about to be a millionaire, if you can't do it, it can't be done." I took my state exam and passed on my first try.

Choosing a brokerage to work for came next. I went to interview with Keller Williams, Century 21 and Tradition Realty. Most of my classmates went with big name real estate brokerages for employment. Even I was close to choosing one myself not knowing any better. Century 21 offered me a sixty/forty percent commission spilt my way. Keller Williams offered me a seventy/thirty percent commission split my way. Tradition Realty offered me a fifty/fifty commission split right down the middle. After interviewing with the three, I noticed something. When I interviewed with Century 21 it was the office manager who interviewed me. When I interviewed with Keller Williams it was the office manager who interviewed me. When I interviewed with Tradition Realty it was the broker himself who interviewed me. After being offered a position at all three brokerages to sell residential homes, I took a week to decide my choice. When I went to the Keller Williams and Century 21's office building they were very stylish in nature. They both had a lot of real estate agents that worked for the brokerages. Both work environments in the offices looked welcoming. When I went to Tradition Realty, there were not a lot of real estate agents that worked for the brokerage. The office was outdated with furniture and styling. There were only two computers that the agents shared. The office definitely was not welcoming to a new agent. During the week of trying to make my mind up on which brokerage I would go work for, I called the broker at Tradition Realty. I told him that I was going to be a real estate broker and owner someday. I asked him if I joined his brokerage would he have an open-door policy with me. I asked him if he would answer questions that I may have about his daily tasks as a broker. He agreed and said yes. I took the lowest paid commission split offered to me when I chose to work for Tradition Realty. But I knew exactly what I was doing.

You have to know where you're going in life so you can decide what's best for you. Everything that glitters is not gold. Receiving more upfront could mean you're losing more at the end. So, the first day on the job I wore some Dockers and a button up shirt to the office. The broker was an older gentleman in his early eighties who took notice of what I was wearing. He called me into his office and stated to me that the dress code was for all males to wear a shirt and tie. He stated to me that you must dress like you're important and people will treat you like you're important. As he stood there in his suit looking just that important, I understood what he meant. From that day on I always wore a shirt and tie when I was working.

The first order of business he stated was to get my phone out and call every person in it. He told me to tell them all that I was now a real estate agent and if they needed assistance with buying or selling their home to give me a call. Then he walked away. I did as I was told and notified everyone in my phone that I was now a real estate agent and to please call me if they decide to buy or sell a home. I went to work for a week and nothing. No leads at all. I just sat at an empty desk. Then one day I said I will make my own marketing materials and market myself. I paid for signs that read "bank owned", "foreclosure" and "HUD List for Free". I scattered them all around town. Next thing you know I had my phone ringing off the hook. I mean I gained about three to five clients a day who decided to make me their Realtor. I started closing deals one after another. I learned from each deal what prospective buyers and sellers wanted when buying or selling a house. They wanted someone they could trust. They wanted someone who showed them they had their interest at heart and not their own. My broker told me at the end of my first year, that in his fifty years of real estate he had never seen any agent learn the business so fast and sell so many houses in their first year. He said the state average sales for a full-time agent was eight to ten houses sold a year. Then he went on to say how I had sold twenty-three.

The next year I added more marketing materials and perfected a system that I could teach other agents. I also received an overwhelming amount of referrals and repeat clients as investors. This allowed me to sell forty-three houses my second year. I repeated similar numbers my third year with forty-four houses sold. My broker was amazed by my performance. Just like that, my three years of being a full-time sales person was over. I sold over one hundred houses in my first three years of real estate. This gave me more than enough real estate experience to enroll in real estate broker school to become a broker.

CHAPTER EIGHT

Right on Schedule

During the first three years, I learned a lot from my broker. I did not ask him a lot of questions during the three years. You see, I learn better by watching. I studied his work ethic, his boss demeanor, daily work assignments and his overall office managing skills. I studied to see what time he arrived and left for the day. I only asked questions when I was puzzled by an answer he would give a fellow agent over a matter. I would want to know his reasoning behind the answer. I truly don't think he knew just how much I learned from him over the three years. I remember when I walked into his office and told him I was going to broker school. He said you have to work at least three years. I told him that I have. He said, "Wow, it's been three years already." I stated, "Yes, it has been, sir." Like a gentleman, he wished me luck with school. I enrolled in real estate broker school on the month of my three-year real estate anniversary. I was in broker school for two and a half months. I actually took my class online. Unlike the real estate sales person school, I quickly found out that broker school would be much harder to graduate from. I was still working full-time at Tradition Realty and going to broker school at night. I would wait for my wife to put the kids to sleep around nine o'clock each day. Then I would log on to my online class. I would do my schooling from nine o'clock at night to midnight every night for two and a half months. It was very hard to stay awake early on. I started to buy big bags of sunflower seeds and I would eat them while I studied. This would keep me up because I was constantly moving, grabbing one and breaking the shells with my teeth. The sunflower seeds were also healthy so I wasn't worried about eating late every night.

I finished real estate broker school and was preparing to take my state exam. During my three years in the real estate business, I had talked to other agents and brokers about broker school, and they all stated how hard the broker state exam was. This made me study for an extra month after completing broker school. I kept the same ritual with the sunflower seeds and studied every night for an additional month from nine until midnight. So, finally

I signed up to take the broker test. The night before the test me and two of my best friends went to a mayoral candidate convention. During the convention it was a who's who of the city. There were doctors, lawyers, politicians, business owners, and real estate brokers in attendance to name just a few. I remember telling my two good friends, who both agreed to come over and work for my brokerage when it opened, that tomorrow I will be a real estate broker. I will have achieved my goal of becoming a real estate broker. Next up would be me opening up my very own real estate brokerage.

So, the next day as I left the house to go take my test, my wife said, "Bye, Mr. Real Estate Broker." I replied, "I'm just minutes away from being one, wish me luck." I got to the testing facility, and it was the same one where I took my state sales person exam three years earlier, which made me feel a little more comfortable. I started the 120-question exam. You are allowed three and half hours to complete the exam. As I made my way thru the exam, my assurance that I would pass on the first try went away more and more. To be honest with you, when I finished the exam, I did not know if I had passed or failed. It was that hard of a test. I have a Bachelor's degree in Science. Let me tell you. I have never taken such a hard test to before. I started to think about how arrogant and cocky I had acted to my family and friends. I could not answer to them that I failed and I had to retake it.

Well, the moment of truth arrived. I called the state employee to let her know I finished. It took me literally three and half hours. She went to my computer and put in a code. All I know is I saw the word "Pass" come up in green letters. I wanted to start dancing and singing. One of the best moments in my life! I was so happy, I called everybody to tell them the good news. My wife was happy and calm with the "I told you so" answer. I went to work the next day and told my broker that I passed my state exam. He congratulated me and wished me the best of luck. He said in his fifty plus years in the real estate business, I was the sixth agent to become a broker and start a company. Moreover, none of them had done it as fast as I did. The greatest compliment he ever gave me was when he said, "I will never find another agent like you." He said I was special. He stated that people like me come around once in a lifetime. With him being the age of eighty-five it meant that much more to me.

So, now it was time for me to open my very own real estate brokerage. I named the company Reach Realty Group. My first choice for the company name was Worldwide International Realty. I quickly changed it when my wife laughed at the name for several days. So, Reach Realty Group it is. I managed to save fourteen thousand dollars and I had a credit card with an eight-thousand-dollar limit. Therefore, with a twenty-two-thousand-dollar budget I started my company. I paid to have the LLC of my company name. Then I bought the domain name reachrealty-group.com. I paid for a logo, and opened bank accounts. I went out and found office space to rent. I bought office furniture and everything else you need to run a business. From an office printer to pens, my twenty-two thousand was getting eaten up fast. Finally, it was complete, and the office looked great. I had a big sign on the wall with Reach Realty Group on it. I had custom rugs with the company logo on them, which truly looked very nice and professional. The stage was set.

I was blessed when I opened my company's doors. I had two of my best friends who are licensed real estate agents join my brokerage. I made both of them my vice-presidents of the company. One a senior vice-president, the other a vice president. I went from working eight hours a day five days a week, to eleven or twelve hours a day six days a week. I was never a coffee drinker. That all changed during my first year of opening the business. I went from not drinking coffee at all to about two or three cups a day. The stress load of the agents' problems can test your nerves. I had been an agent for three years at Tradition Realty and I never gave my broker one problem to solve. In the first year of being open for business both of my trusted friends made costly mistakes. The most severe mistake was having a client purchase a house that was forfeited to the county for unpaid taxes. The deal should have never closed. I learned a valuable lesson with that problem. The les son I learned was to never trust anyone in business. Many times we all put too much trust in people. Since that day not one file has closed in my office without me giving the go ahead first. I was very lucky with that situation. I was able to call an investor to buy the house out of the tax auction and resell it back to the client.

There were a lot of ups and down that year. I was still selling a lot of houses but there were three months where no other agent sold a house. This put a little more financial burden on me than I had expected. After that three-month period things picked up and I ended the year in the black for income earned.

After my first year as a real estate company owner, I decided to move into the next real estate market and become a landlord. The second year in business I bought three fixer upper houses. One by one I went in and rehabbed the property. I would have my friends come by to help me paint and fix minor re pairs on our one day off, Sunday. I fixed one up then rented the property out. I would take the money the tenant paid to move in one property and invest it into the next one. I was able to do this by not charging a security deposit. If you charge a tenant a security deposit to move into a rental, the funds must be deposited in a bank account and not touched until the tenants move out. I would charge first and last month rent up front to move in. This allowed me to get the same amount of money most landlords received but could only spend half. I would take the funds and start on the next property including the rent that was monthly paid as well. When I finally finished the rehab, and found tenants for all three properties, I bought one more and repeated the process, including the house I lived in, which brought my total to five houses I owned now.

By this time, three years had passed and the real estate market went up by forty to eighty percent. The values of the five properties was now worth around a combined price of four hundred thousand dollars. I was very pleased with the value amounts; I paid about a hundred and twenty thou sand dollars for all five including the rehab work. In three years to turn one hundred and twenty thousand into four hundred thousand is very impressive I would say. Even though I have seen other clients make more in a shorter time period, I was very happy with my real estate portfolio.

During that year, I had my company business evaluation. After three years of profiting making a combined total of around two hundred and seventy-five thousand dollars, my company was now worth over six hundred thousand dollars. At the time, I had over eighty thousand dollars in cash in my savings account. The only debt I owed was my student loan bill of roughly thirty-five thousand dollars, on which I made monthly payments. After I deducted my liabilities from my assets, I had a net worth of more than a million dollars. I did it!!! Yes, I had become a self-made millionaire.

I remember thinking to myself: Wow! In less than seven years I had reached my goal of becoming a millionaire. I was very proud of myself. My goal was to become a millionaire in ten years or less and the goal was completed. To be honest with you, that same year I read an article in a magazine and the topic was, why most millionaires don't feel rich. I read the article and agreed with most of it. You see, most people think that if you're a millionaire you have a million dollars in your bank account. This is very much not true. The majority of millionaire's money is usually tied up in assets. By the time someone has a million dollars in cash in their bank account, this person is most likely a multi-millionaire. I agreed with the article because although I was years out from the last time I worried about paying a bill or buying groceries, I could not go out and buy a Lamborghini, helicopter or mega yacht. I could not go on vacations for months at a time. I still had to very much so wake up six days of week and go to work. So, I did feel very blessed and fortunate but not financially rich. It was only when my wife pointed out to me to stop and think about our lifestyle. She pointed out how I started a company that was now very successful, that we had no unfulfilled wants or needs. We are literally living the lives we prayed and dreamed about. That's when it finally set in that I had made it.

I followed the instructions in this book and now I have financial freedom to live my life to the fullest.

I recommend you set high goals for yourself but make sure you stop to appreciate how far you have come during your transformation. What I think happens is as you climb the ladder to becoming a millionaire, you secretly push up the meters and bounds for what is financially successful to you. That is why you have billionaires who keep working hard every day. You wonder why they don't stop working. It's because they fall in love with the game of success. If you become a billionaire you will meet other billionaires with two or three times more money than you. Maybe even more than that. So now you set another benchmark that you want to reach. If you have a strong competitive side to you and you are driven by success, the game never ends until you're the richest man on earth. Even then the game will be to stay the richest man on earth.

NESAHN ROBINSON

www.ingramcontent.com/pod-product-compliance
Lightning Source LLC
Chambersburg PA
CBHW021113210326
41598CB00017B/1436